YOUR GIFT FROM GOD

IS IN YOUR NAME

DELORES MARIE GRIGGS

YOUR GIFT FROM GOD

IS IN YOUR NAME

Rare Pearls Publishing
P.O Box 279050
Sacramento, CA 95827

ISBN: 978-0-9982256-0-9
Delores Marie Griggs © 2019
Library of Congress Control Number: 2019907403

www.rarepearlspublishing.com

All rights reserved under the International Copyright Law. Contents and cover may not be reproduced or transmitted in any form, or by any means, electronic or mechanical, including photocopying, recording, or any information storage and retrieval system, in whole or in part, without the express written consent of the author.

Definitions are from the 1913 Webster's Dictionary in the Public Domain.

The Scripture quotations are from the King James Bible, Thomas Nelson, 1972.

The population statistics came from the United States Census Bureau International Data Base, July 1, 2015.

The chapters have Scriptures at the end of this book, and anyone can review them to verify the author's statements.

This Author is not a Theologian; therefore, this book is from a layman's perspective.

Book Cover Design: Delores Marie Griggs

Dedication

To my late parents William Griggs, who named me, and Amanda Atkinson. Both encouraged me to pursue my dreams.

To my twin sister Denise, who supported this process with me.

I am eternally grateful to each of them.

Prologue

- To anyone contemplating *Suicide*, consider this: Your name is important to God as He made you unique like Him. God has gifts, benefits, and a purpose for you to share with the rest of the world. We all need you! This book is for you.

- To anyone who does not believe in Jesus nor ever felt the need to accept Him as your Savior, know this, He believes in you! You are just as important to God as He has gifts and benefits with your name on them. Keep an open mind as you read this book.

- To anyone who left the church because someone hurt you, come back. Remember how important you, your name, and your gifts are to God.

- To anyone whose loved one or friends rejected you because you became a Christian, remember, God loves you more than anyone and promises never to abandon you.

- To the Christian who attends church regularly but never felt like you belonged or are not engaged in the ministry, remember, you and your name are extra special to God. He has a plan for you within the church.

Call unto me,
and I will answer thee,
and show thee great and mighty things,
which thou knowest not.

Jeremiah 33:3

Contents

	Page
Prologue	5
Contents	7
Introduction	8
Chapter 1 — A Good Name	13
Chapter 2 — Order A Natural & A Spiritual Order	18
Chapter 3 — God's Blueprint for Names	20
Chapter 4 — Names Are to Be Honored	24
Chapter 5 — Names with Special Gifts	28
Chapter 6 — Name Changes for Positive Results	42
Chapter 7 — Names with Negative Results	50
Chapter 8 — Most Negative Name Changes	63
Chapter 9 — Something to Think About	71
Chapter 10 — God Introduced His Name: Jehovah, 1st Name of the Godhead	74
Chapter 11 — God Introduced His Name: Jesus, 2nd Name of the Godhead	77
Chapter 12 — God Introduced His Name: The Holy Spirit, 3rd Name of the Godhead.	83
Chapter 13 — Final Evidence	89
Chapter 14 — How Do I Find Out What My Name Means	93
Chapter 15 — Conclusion	103
Scriptures	109
About the Author	127

Introduction

Do you know there are over 7 billion people alive in the world today?

Do you know each person has something in common?

- First, everyone has a *Name*.
- Secondly, everyone has a *Natural Gift* or employment which can be nurtured and developed over time by education, research, and practice.
- Third, anyone who has accepted Jesus Christ as their Savior has a *Spiritual Gift* from God they will discover as they read the Scripture and become more familiar with Him.

I will demonstrate how God gives a Natural and Spiritual Gift to each of us and how we can find our gifts in our name.

Names

Names are essential to identify us whether we were born into our family or adopted. We can find names recorded on birth certificates, church records, and family bibles. Many parents named us after themselves or our ancestors. Other names changed due to marriage and are on marriage licenses.

Not only can we be identified by our name, but today, our fingerprints and a blood/DNA test can confirm our identity. Both recognize us from any other person, even if we have the same name.

The Scripture states:

- Each birth is a gift from God.
- Before our birth, God had a plan and purpose for each of us. He gave us powerful gifts and abilities in our names, like the abilities in His name.
- God wants everyone to know that we are loved, unique, and adored by Him regardless of our life circumstances.

Natural Gifts

In addition to our names, each of us has a Natural gift when choosing our career. Some of us will follow our parent's careers as police officers, doctors, nurses, athletes, or actors. Others are naturally gifted singers, musicians, and artists. However, to be competent in any career, all require continued education, research, and practice.

The Scripture states that God:

- Planned for everyone to enjoy their life.
- Requires everyone to get wisdom and knowledge, both Naturally and Spiritually.
- Wants us to get an understanding through the practice of our knowledge learned.

Spiritual Gifts

The Holy Spirit gives spiritual gifts to each person who has accepted Jesus as their Lord and Savior. These gifts exist to maintain the unity, function, and beliefs of Christians worldwide. It doesn't matter what country we live in, our race or nationality, because collectively, we are called the body of Jesus Christ.

These gifts include insight and revelation of the Scripture, which is our power. Jesus won all of His battles by knowing the Scripture. When we study and understand the Scripture, we can "walk on water" during the storms of our lives or the temptations in our lives.

Names are important because the Scripture states at the beginning of human creation, God created a man and named him Adam.

He was made in God's unique image and had God's breath within him.

In Adam's name, his Natural gift was employment. God instructed him to name all of the animals He made before creating him, plus work and take care of the Garden of Eden where he lived.

Adam's Spiritual gift was his daily communication with God. God also gave him the unique ability to be creative, like Him, and he became the father of all humans.

Realizing Adam shouldn't be alone, God created a female for him, and Adam named her Woman. God created her from one of Adam's ribs; therefore, *God referred to them both as Adam.*

As Adams' wife, her Natural gift was to work side by side with him, as one, and her Spiritual gift was daily communication with God too. God also gave her the unique gift of creativity. She eventually became the mother of all humans. God designed them to obey Him and live forever. Giving Natural and Spiritual gifts was also God's plan for humanity.

One day, God was looking for Adam. He

called *his name*; however, he and his wife were hiding because they disobeyed His commandment.

When God questioned them, He found out that they *listened to and obeyed someone other than Him.* Both had an excuse for being disobedient, but God expelled them from the Garden of Eden forever!

At the end of time, the Scripture states that God will call each of us, by name, to see if we were also obedient or rebellious against His plans for our lives. Will we be hiding and have an excuse for not obeying Him too?

In this book, each of us will discover how to find the original plan and purpose God intended for our lives, both Naturally and Spiritually, just as He did with Adam and his wife. Therefore, I firmly believe <u>Your Gift from God is in Your Name.</u>

For I know the thoughts that I think towards you, said the Lord, thoughts of peace, and not of evil, to give you an expected end.

Jeremiah 29:11

Chapter One

A Good Name

A good name is rather to be chosen than great riches.

Proverbs 22:1

We know or have heard of people who started their business by only using their initials, first name, or last name. Sometimes, they used two or more names joined together for their business, and they were successful with great reviews.

You will find hundreds of people with the same name on the Internet and various media sources. If you are a genealogist, you can trace families back hundreds and thousands of years and find people with the same name. Can multiple people with the same name have different gifts and talents? The answer is yes. Whatever gift(s) God gives us, *we will reach different audiences.*

In the Old Testament Scripture, an example of a person who had a good name and followed God's plan for his life was a young shepherd boy named David. His responsibilities were to keep and care for the sheep which belonged to his father.

In his youth, David developed an intimate relationship with God through praise, worship, songs, prayer, and meditation. In turn, God blessed David with the gift of successfully caring for the flock and the physical strength to fight off wild animals that tried to attack his father's sheep. Being a shepherd was a hard life; however, from these experiences, David developed leadership skills, organizational skills, and fighting skills.

As a young man, David was anointed king over the Israelites. God used David's skills and experiences as a shepherd to become an excellent leader, strategist, warrior, and king over God's people.

King David also interacted with *all* of the people in his kingdom, and they loved him! One example was when he returned the Sacred Ark of the Covenant back home. The people celebrated with music, singing, dancing, and the *king danced with them as well.* Then, before they left to go home, the king prayed for them and gave them all food gifts.

King David wasn't a perfect man, but he had excellent wisdom and a good name. David was also blessed to live a long time.

***

Another person with a good name was Solomon, King David's young son and successor to his throne. When the Priest anointed him as king, the people celebrated all day with music, dancing and the king provided sacrificial burnt offerings to the Lord.

Later, while Solomon was sleeping, God appeared in his dream and asked him what he needed from Him. The young king requested wisdom, knowledge, and an understanding heart to discern between his kingdom's good and bad people.

God was pleased with Solomon's request for wisdom and knowledge. He told Solomon since he did not ask for wealth, a long life, or the death of his enemies, He would bless him with wisdom and wealth like no other king. God also blessed the king to live a long time. As a result, King Solomon became known worldwide as the wisest and richest king.

***

In Summary, the Scripture states, "When the righteous are in authority, the people rejoice." At the mention of their names, people will say good words about them during their lifetime and years after their deaths.

Yet, some people have a good name, are rich in wisdom, but lack financial resources due to something beyond their control. They could have been born handicapped, had an unforeseen sudden illness, an accident, and cannot work. Still, they must use wisdom to find ways to feed, clothe, shelter, support themselves and their families.

One example is when Jesus told the story of two men, a poor man named Lazarus and a rich man. Lazarus did not fare well in life. He was disabled, full of sores, and had to beg to support himself.

Even though poor Lazarus had a disability, he had faith and trusted God daily to supply his needs. Every day, people in town carried him to the rich man's home, so he could beg for the crumbs which fell from his table.

Eventually, poor Lazarus died, and the Angels peacefully carried him away to Father Abraham's bosom, in heaven. Despite his circumstances, Lazarus trusted God, and in God's sight, Lazarus had a good name.

However, the rich man was very selfish, and every day, he lived lavishly, wore expensive clothing, and ate very well. He trusted only himself, his wealth, and his luxurious lifestyle, but He did not honor God.

One day, the selfish rich man died too; however, he woke up tormented in hell! He looked and saw Lazarus far away in the bosom of Abraham and selfishly cried for mercy! He begged Abraham to send Lazarus to bring him water to cool his tongue! Abraham, however, denied his request and informed him that neither of them could cross their eternal boundaries!

In Summary, this story reveals how poor people honor and trust God to meet their needs, regardless if they need assistance from others. Others use their time to volunteer and their finances to provide for the poor or those with extreme hardships. They all are examples of people with good names.

Jesus stated that if anyone assists someone in need, they are actually providing it to Him. He loves those who help serve others and promises to repay them during their lifetime and when He resurrects His faithful people from death.

Chapter Two

Order: A Natural & Spiritual Order

To understand why we exist, we must go back to the beginning of time and consider God's original plan for each of us. It is a Natural Order and a Spiritual Order.

Natural Order

It doesn't matter if you are born male or female, rich or poor, your race, or what country you live in. There are absolutes about everyone. All have:

- Biological parents.
- A day of birth.
- A Name.
- 24 hours each day.
- Four seasons each year: Spring, Summer, Fall, and Winter.
- A Natural gift and
- An expiration date or a day to die.

God gave everyone the Natural Order to work and manage their life, career, and family; therefore, obtaining a solid education can lead to a good job and a long career. For example, an Architect must know many laws, codes, math, designs, planning, and technology to correctly develop lands, build homes, buildings, stadiums, and shopping malls worldwide.

Spiritual Order

Everyone has:

- A Spiritual gift from God *if* you have accepted Jesus as your Savior.
- After death, a day of judgment, and
- Eternal life with *or* without God.

Through Jesus, God gave us the Spiritual Order to complete our spiritual assignment with Him, our local church, and with our fellow man.

Although Jesus is the new agreement between God and man, God still wants us to love Him first, then follow the Ten Commandments and the Golden Rule.

The Ten Commandments are for us to live a life pleasing to God, and the Golden Rule is for our relationship with others. Therefore, God commanded that we treat our fellow man as we would treat ourselves.

Chapter Three

God's Blueprint for Names

When God created the first man, He blew His breath into him like CPR. The man became alive, a living soul, with thoughts, emotions, and God's awareness, his Creator. God named him Adam.

God then formed a mate for Adam, and using the exact naming blueprint of God, Adam named her Woman. They were innocent, naked, and not ashamed.

God gave them dominion over all He created and told them that they could freely eat the fruit of any tree; however, He *commanded* them not to eat "of the tree of the knowledge of good and evil," as they would "surely die."

God gave them the gift of free will, but unfortunately, both chose to disobey God's commandment and ate the fruit. ***Eating the fruit poisoned their blood and changed their DNA, making them unable to live forever or in the Garden of Eden anymore.*** So, God made them leave and sent them into the wilderness to fend for themselves until they died.

While in the wilderness, Adam renamed his wife Eve, and they began having children. Eve also followed God's naming pattern and named their first child Cain and their second child Abel.

Their children had Natural gifts and talents which developed over time. For example, Cain became a farmer and grew vegetables, and Abel was a shepherd over his flock of sheep.

God gave both men Spiritual gifts, which were commandments on how to honor and worship Him, and in turn, He would forgive their sins. God told them He would be pleased with them if they followed the same example He demonstrated to their parents when He forgave them. He told them to bring Him the *blood* of a pure and unbred animal as a sacrifice, which was *necessary* to make restitution to atone for their sin. (to be discussed in a later chapter)

Abel was obedient and honored God's instructions by sacrificing his best animal from his flock and bringing its blood to God. God was pleased with him and accepted his gift.

God, however, did not accept Cain's offering as he disrespected God and disobeyed His instructions. Cain brought the best of his vegetables; however, vegetables could never atone for sin.

Cain became incredibly angry that God did not accept his gift; however, God explained that He would receive his gift if he brought Him what was required. Additionally, God told Cain to use his free will to control himself, or the Spirit of Anger would destroy him.

Still, in a jealous rage, Cain refused to control himself and killed Abel, his innocent brother! This violent act was the first murder and death in human history.

When God asked Cain where Abel was, Cain defiantly said, "I know not! Am I my brother's keeper?" God, however, told Cain that He knew he murdered him, as Abel's blood was crying to Him from the ground! Cain immediately knew he was in trouble! He remembered that God said, "Life is in the blood."

As punishment for murdering Abel, God banished Cain from His presence forever! Cain became a fugitive and a vagabond, and his name is *forever* synonymous with his poor attitude towards God, lying and murdering his brother.

In one day, Eve lost both sons. However, due to God's love and mercy, He blessed her to get pregnant again. She gave birth to another son, and following the naming blueprint of God, Eve named her baby Seth.

Chapter Four

Names Are to be Honored

Natural Realm

In the Old and New Testaments of the Bible, God honored many people. The following seven stories are examples of some of them.

In the Old Testament, God promised a man named Abram that He would honor and bless him with many descendants. Abram, however, was 75 years old and Sarai, his wife, was also old and barren.

God further said that He would bless him and make his name great, but first, he had to leave his relatives and move to another land. By simple faith, Abram believed in what God said. Later, God changed his name to Abraham, meaning "father of many nations."

Abraham left, and just as God promised, God honored Abraham with many descendants (to be discussed more in-depth in Chapter Six).

Unfortunately, many of Abraham's descendants continuously sinned and disobeyed God's commandments. For their rebellion, God allowed the Egyptians to defeat them and enslave them for over 400 years. They endured backbreaking labor and repeatedly prayed to God to free them.

***

Secondly, God honored a man named Moses and instructed him to deliver Abraham's descendants from Egyptian slavery. God told him to lead the people to the land God initially promised to give to Abraham. By faith, Moses obeyed. After numerous challenges and miracles, the Egyptian Pharaoh finally released them.

Once the Hebrews were free to leave Egypt, God gave Moses the Ten Commandments to teach them how to honor, worship, and obey Him. These commandments explained how to live life responsibly and are still in effect for all people today.

***

Third, when Moses died, God honored a man named Joshua to be Moses' successor. He told him to finish leading the Hebrews into the Promised Land and not be afraid as He would be with him as He was with Moses. By faith, Joshua obeyed. Even though he also had numerous challenges, he eventually led them into the promised land.

The Hebrews settled into the land, and for the rest of his life, Joshua lived in peace.

***

Fourth, God honored a prophet named Isaiah to declare a future event. Isaiah prophesied that a son would be born to a virgin, and the baby's name would be Immanuel, meaning *God with us*. This one event was pre-ordained to bring humanity back into a right relationship with God.

***

Fifth, in the New Testament, God sent an Angel to inform a young girl named Mary that God wanted to honor her by giving birth to His Son. The Angel told her to name the baby Jesus. Mary, however, said she was a virgin. The Angel advised her that the power of the Holy Spirit would overshadow her to cause her pregnancy, just like at the beginning of time when God overshadowed the universe and created all things. By simple faith, Mary believed what the Angel said, and as Isaiah prophesied 700 years earlier, Mary became pregnant with Jesus.

***

Sixth, God honored a man named Joseph, who was Mary's fiancé; however, Joseph discovered she was pregnant, but not by him. Joseph was a reasonable man; therefore, rather than humiliating her in public, he decided to quietly terminate their engagement. An Angel, however, appeared to Joseph in a dream and told him that God was the father of Mary's baby and proceed with the marriage. The Angel also instructed him to name the baby Jesus, and by faith, Joseph obeyed. Since Joseph's Natural gift was employment as a carpenter, he could adequately provide for Mary and Jesus' earthly needs.

***

In the New Testament, the disciples asked Jesus what proper name to use when praying to God, the Spirit, whom they could not see. He told them to *honor His name, Father.* Since God is the Creator of heaven, earth, humanity, and all things in the world, His name should be honored.

***

In Summary, to all believers, when God sees you, He will honor you as His children. The Scripture also states that God will honor each believer on Judgment Day by giving them a brand-new name.

Chapter Five

Names with Special Gifts

God specifically ordained Jesus and ordinary men and women to usher in a new agreement between God and man, now known as the New Testament. God used an elderly married couple, Zacharias, his wife Elizabeth, and their son John, then Mary, Joseph, Peter, and Paul to complete this purpose.

God, for example, sent an Angel to an elderly Priest named Zacharias and told him that his wife Elizabeth, who was both barren and elderly, would soon have a baby boy. The Angel instructed Zacharias to name the baby John and that John's birth would bring joy to them, plus rejoicing to others.

The Angel informed him that while their baby was still in his mother's womb, the Presence of God's Holy Spirit would enter him. Also, John would be great in the eyes of God, and as an adult, he would influence many in Israel to stop worshipping idols and return to worshipping God.

When Elizabeth was six months pregnant, Mary, who was pregnant with Jesus, visited her.

However, as soon as Mary greeted Elizabeth, her baby immediately leaped in her womb, and the Presence of God's Holy Spirit entered both Elizabeth and her baby. After John was born, the power of the Holy Spirit also entered Zacharias.

When John became an adult, God gave him the unique gift of preaching to the Jews that the Messiah was coming to save them from their inherited sinful nature. He encouraged them to prepare for His coming by repenting of their sin and being water baptized.

John additionally told them that when the Messiah came, *the Messiah would baptize all believers too;* however, it would be with the precious gift of His Holy Spirit, Who would reside within them and guide them for life.

Once they believed his message, he baptized them. Therefore, he is also known as John the Baptist.

***

Jesus was another example of a name with extraordinary gifts. He grew up as an average child; however, He realized that He was different from other children and learned that God was His biological Father.

At age 12, for example, after a Passover celebration in Jerusalem, His parents were returning home and assumed that Jesus was with other family members or friends, but He wasn't. So, thinking He was lost, they returned to Jerusalem to look for Him.

After three days of searching, they found Him in the Synagogue, sitting among the teachers and elders, listening and asking questions. His parents noticed that all who heard Him were astonished at His answers and understanding of the Scripture.

Mary reprimanded Jesus for not asking permission to stay in Jerusalem, but He replied, "I must be about my Father's business." Still, He obeyed, and they all returned home. Mary, however, quietly remembered His response. According to the Scripture, as Jesus matured, He increased in wisdom and favor, both with God and man.

As an adult, Jesus knew one of His Spiritual gifts, as God's Son, was to offer His body as a *final blood sacrifice for the sin of all people*. God no longer wanted animals' blood as a sacrifice for the sin of His people, the Jews. Now, He wanted *all nationalities' blood/DNA cleansed* and to receive the forgiveness of their sin, *but only through the blood of Jesus.*

Before beginning His ministry gift, He first went to John the Baptist to be baptized by him. Jesus, however, didn't need forgiveness of sin as the Scripture states He never sinned, nor was He born in a state of evil or sin like the rest of humanity. (to be discussed in a later chapter)

Once Jesus was baptized, God filled Him with the Presence of His Holy Spirit. Then God spoke from heaven, confirming that Jesus was His Son, and He was pleased with Him for accepting His earthy mission.

Another one of Jesus' gifts was teaching. For example, He taught large crowds from Galilee to Jerusalem, Judea, the Decapolis, and the region beyond Jordan. People followed Him and were astonished to learn that the only requirement to be forgiven of their sin was to recognize Him as the Son of God and accept Him as their Savior.

In one of the lessons, Jesus taught that **God did not send him to judge them** but **forgive them** of their inherited rebellious nature, named sin. Further, He assured them that they did not have to fear death anymore as He promised all believers that they would also be resurrected and spend eternity with God after their deaths.

Finally, during a teachable moment with just one man, Jesus explained that salvation, or accepting Him as Savior, meant a new birth or *"Spiritually" born again.* Jesus confirmed no one could enter the Kingdom of God nor receive any of God's benefits without this new birth.

Another lesson He taught was the Beatitudes, also known as the Sermon on the Mount, in which He explained that life might not always be easy, but they still could live a peaceful, blessed life by having faith in God and obeying His Word.

Healing was also another one of Jesus' unique gifts. When He placed His hands on the sick and prayed for them, the power of God flowed through Him, healing them from their diseases, pain, demonic spirits or mental illness, and seizures.

The only time Jesus could not heal anyone was in Nazareth, his hometown. First, they refused to believe He was the prophesied Messiah. Secondly, they said He was only a man, and they knew Him as a local carpenter's son. Jesus, however, was not moved by their unbelief and stated that a prophet does not have honor in His hometown.

So, He continued healing in other towns.

The most unique gift given to Jesus was after His burial. Three days later, He rose from the dead and permanently defeated Satan's dominion and grip on humanity. Jesus took away Satan's ability to constantly *torment* humanity by *terrifying* us of death, *fearing* the unknown, and the excruciating thought of going to hell for eternity. Jesus' resurrection reaffirmed to all believers that they too would be resurrected.

The Scripture, however, states that those who refuse to accept Jesus during their lifetime will also be resurrected *but will follow Satan to hell for eternity.*

***

Another person given a special gift was Simon, later known as Peter, a disciple of Jesus. (to be discussed in a later chapter)

Peter preached, only to the Jews, that Jesus was the Messiah. For centuries, Prophets prophesized that a Messiah was coming to set up a new kingdom. Many Jews erroneously *thought* that Jesus' new kingdom would be on earth and ensure the Romans would never rule over them again. Most were disappointed to learn that Jesus meant a Spiritual Kingdom; however, some became converts.

The Jewish Priest did not like that Jesus was becoming popular with the people, so they took advantage of their disappointment and spread misinformation about Him. Ultimately, the people agreed that Jesus was a fraud, and they insisted on His death.

After Jesus rose from the grave and ascended back into heaven, God gave Peter a vision, while he was asleep, of a sheet coming down from heaven with unclean animals in it. A Voice instructed him to eat the animals. Peter, however, answered, "Not so, Lord, for I have never eaten anything that is common or unclean." The Voice replied and said, "What God hath cleansed, do not call it common." Peter awakened but was unsure what the vision meant.

At the same time as Peter's vision, God sent an Angel to a Roman officer named Cornelius. When Cornelius saw the Angel coming to him, he was terrified! However, the Angel calmed him down by telling him that God heard his prayers, and his giving to the poor was a memorial to Him.

The Angel told Cornelius to send three men to

find Peter, and Peter would tell him what to do.

After the men found Peter, they told him that Cornelius honored God, respected the Jews, and Cornelius asked them to find him.

When Peter arrived at Cornelius' home, Peter told him it was against the Jewish law for a Jew to enter a non-Jew/Gentile's house. Cornelius, however, shared with him about the Angel visitation, and he and his household were waiting to hear what Peter needed to tell them. Then Peter understood the vision God gave him, which was, ***no man God created was unclean.***

Peter entered Cornelius' home and explained the good news that God sent Jesus, His only son, as a blood sacrifice to forgive men of their sin. Further, once anyone accepted Jesus as their Savior, after death, they would spend eternity with God in heaven.

While Peter was still talking, the Holy Spirit's Presence entered Cornelius and all of his household. Peter was stunned because he witnessed them praising and worshipping God in other languages (tongues), the same way Peter and the disciples experienced in Jerusalem!

Cornelius and his entire household were the first non-Jews that Peter preached about Jesus. They all accepted Jesus as their Savior, and Peter baptized them.

Peter returned to Jerusalem and preached to the Jews that Jesus was indeed the Messiah. The people, numbered in thousands, listened to him and were grief-stricken that they agreed to His death. They begged Peter to explain how God would forgive them!

Peter explained that the only requirement was to repent of their sin and be baptized in Jesus' name, as their baptism was a symbol of being buried and resurrected with Him. That day three thousand people accepted Jesus.

As Peter and the other disciples continued preaching, five thousand more people accepted Jesus as their Savior. The new converts were later named Christians.

***

Lastly, another person with a special gift was a Jew named Saul, later renamed Paul. (to be discussed in a later chapter)

Teaching the Torah, the Jewish Law, was his Natural gift. Some examples of the Torah taught that justification with God was through the Ten Commandments, moral laws, and yearly animal blood sacrifices for the forgiveness of their sin.

Initially, Saul hated the Jewish converts because he believed that their message of a new agreement between God and man was blasphemous and contrary to Jewish law. Nor did he believe that in place of animals' blood, Jesus' blood was the final sacrifice for the forgiveness of their sin. Many times, Saul received permission from the High Priest to pursue the Jewish converts to arrest and imprison them.

One day as Saul traveled to Damascus to pursue the Jewish converts to imprison them, a bright light from heaven blinded him, and he fell off his horse. The Voice from the Light asked Saul why he was persecuting Him. A terrified Saul asked the Voice to identify himself and the Voice replied, "I am Jesus of Nazareth." Saul, astonished and trembling, asked Jesus what He wanted from him! Jesus told him to continue to Damascus, and what He wanted would be revealed to him.

At the same time Saul was blinded by the light, Jesus revealed in a vision to another disciple, named Ananias, to find Saul and pray for the restoration of his sight. At first, Ananias refused because he didn't trust Saul, and he knew Saul was responsible for arresting many new Jewish converts. Jesus, however, told him that He chose Saul to preach the good news about salvation to the Gentiles, kings, and the children of Israel.

Ananias obeyed, found Saul, prayed for him, and Saul's sight was restored. Saul accepted Jesus as his Savior, received the Holy Spirit's infilling, and the disciple baptized him.

Since Saul was a scholar of the Jewish Law, he was qualified to compare and demonstrate in the Law that Jesus was the prophesied Messiah. However, when the Jewish converts learned that Saul converted to Christianity, they became outraged and thought it was a trick to harm them! They did not trust him and made plans to kill him; however, Saul heard about their plans and immediately left town!

Saul, who was Jewish, was also a Roman citizen, and His Jewish name Saul, plus his Roman name Paul were interchangeable; therefore, he began using his Roman name. However, the converted Jews still did not believe him, so Paul started teaching to the Gentiles (non-Jews); however, the Gentiles had no idea that they needed a Savior.

One example of Paul's teaching to the Gentiles was when he went to the city of Antioch. The people believed in many Gods, including an unknown God. Paul's teaching about Jesus was unheard of, so they asked him to come back the following week to continue teaching.

Paul returned the next week, and most of the entire city returned to hear his message. Paul taught them that accepting Jesus meant that each of them could receive forgiveness of their inherited sin, and after death, they would spend eternity with only **One God**, the Creator of Heaven and Earth.

The people were ecstatic to hear this good news and wanted to know how they could receive salvation! Paul told them that salvation was simple and said, "Believe in the Lord Jesus, and you will be saved." Immediately, many of them received Jesus as their Savior.

Paul taught three things for many years. First, regardless of anyone's race or nationality, the ***forgiveness* of one's sin was for *all people***. Secondly, it was needless to work for salvation as it is ***a free gift from God***. Third, ***no one could receive salvation for being just a good person***. He pointed out in Scripture that Jesus said, *"There is none good but One, that is, God."*

Paul wrote to many believers how to live their lives once they became Christians. Paul's writings are in the Bible, known as the New Testament.

Finally, Paul suffered many ills and mishaps after converting to Christianity; however, he brought many people to faith in Jesus during his ministry.

***

In Summary, all humanity inherited Adam and Eve's poisoned blood (DNA), which needed cleansing. Their tainted blood caused each of us to be born in their state of disobedience or sin, and this state made us unable to live forever, or in heaven, just as Adam and Eve could no longer live forever, or in the beautiful Garden of Eden.

Jesus' special gift was to destroy this poison and heal us, giving us ***a pure-blood transfusion*** that allowed us to be ***Spiritually born again***. When we accept the gift of Jesus as Savior, we can live with Him in heaven forever.

Additionally, God wanted His Spiritual children, His real treasure, to assist Him in ushering in this new birth. And through our unique gifts, we allow God to work *through us*, as He did through Jesus. His goal is to successfully redeem humanity, His children, back to Him (to be discussed in a later chapter)

These examples of people's names with special gifts demonstrate how Christianity began and developed over time. Except for Jesus, these people were not perfect, but it was proof that God gave and still gives numerous opportunities to each believer to fulfill the unique gifts He has for them.

The Scripture also states that God knew what special gift(s) He would give each person before we were born.

For thou hast possessed my reins; thou hast covered me in my mother's womb...

Psalms 139:13

Chapter Six

Names Changes for Positive Results

Some stories demonstrated why God changed names for positive results in the Old and New Testaments of the Bible.

One example was Abram, who was 75 years old when God appeared and asked him to make a Sacred agreement with Him. For the arrangement to be successful, God told Abram to leave his relatives and go to a land where He wanted to bless him. Further, He would make his name great, make his family a great nation, and He would bless him to be a blessing to all families of the earth. Abram agreed, and by faith, left his relatives and arrived in Canaan, now known as Israel. Once there, God told him that the land now belonged to him and his descendants forever.

When Abram was 99 years old, God revisited him and told him that he and his wife would have a baby the following year. God *changed his name to Abraham,* meaning *a father* of many nations, and changed his wife's name to *Sarah*, meaning a mother of many nations and kings.

Abraham laughed at the thought of fathering a child with his wife as Sarah was 89 years old and unable to have children. God instructed Abraham to name the baby Isaac, and He too would establish his covenant with Isaac and his descendants.

The following year, when Abraham was 100 years old, 90-year-old Sarah gave birth to their promised son. As God instructed, they named him Isaac.

In Summary, Abraham's faith in God and God renaming him changed his life. Since then, Abraham's known as the *Father of Faith* and Isaac's birth guaranteed Gods' covenant promise.

***

When Isaac became an adult, he married Rebekah, and later on, they found out she was pregnant with twins. God revealed that the twins would eventually become two nations; however, the elder twin would serve the younger twin. This revelation was against a father's custom of giving his first-born son a double portion of his property and blessing.

The first twin was red and hairy like a garment, and they named him Esau. When the younger twin was born, he had his hand on Esau's heel, and they named him Jacob, meaning supplanter or one who deceives another.

As the twins matured, Esau became an outdoorsman and skilled hunter, but Jacob preferred staying home and living indoors. Isaac loved Esau the most, but Rebekah loved Jacob more.

One day, Jacob saw Esau returning home from hunting and saw an opportunity to undermine him for his birthright blessing. Jacob was cooking stew and knew Esau wanted to eat. Esau, exhausted and extremely hungry, begged Jacob to share his food.

Jacob told Esau to sell the firstborn birthright to him, and he would give him some of his food. Esau said that the birthright would be of no use to him if he didn't eat right now! Then, Jacob made Esau swear he would give up his birthright, and he hastily agreed.

The Scripture states that Esau despised his birthright, yet Jacob valued the blessing more. Esau gave away his birthright for food, which *he thought* would be an instant pleasure, much like Adam and Eve in the Garden of Eden.

Their father, Isaac, now old, almost blind, and nearing death, summoned Esau and told him he wanted to give him his birthright blessing. Isaac asked him to go hunting first, and afterward, fix him a meal. Esau immediately obeyed.

Rebekah overheard them and persuaded Jacob into deceiving his father for the blessing. For their plan to succeed, Rebekah took Esau's clothes and put them on Jacob so he could smell like Esau. She also put goat hair on Jacob's hands and neck to feel hairy like Esau. Finally, Rebekah cooked the food Isaac wanted as she knew Isaac couldn't see or taste the difference if she or Esau cooked it.

Jacob went to his father, dressed like Esau, and Isaac passed the firstborn blessing onto him, and by custom, it was irrevocable. Therefore, Rebekah and Jacob's deception succeeded.

When Esau returned home from hunting, he found out that Jacob received the firstborn blessing. Horrified, Esau cried in anguish! He knew the blessing was irrevocable and angrily said that Jacob's name was correct as one who deceives! Jacob tricked him twice and swore he would kill Jacob once their father died!

Informed of Esau's plot to kill Jacob, Rebekah deceitfully asked Isaac to send Jacob to her brother's house under the pretense of finding a suitable wife. Even though it was far from home, Isaac agreed, and Jacob left immediately!

After many years living with his uncle, the Lord told Jacob to return home, but he was afraid Esau still wanted to kill him! However, by faith, he obeyed.

When Jacob left and came closer to home, he sent his family ahead of him, hoping that it would appease Esau's anger when he saw them.

At nightfall and alone, Jacob was praying when suddenly, an unknown Man appeared! Fearfully, Jacob and the Man began wrestling and struggling all night! Finally, at dawn, the Man dislocated Jacob's hip and shouted, "Let me go!" However, Jacob screamed back, "I will not let you go until you bless me!"

The Man stopped fighting and asked Jacob for his name. Jacob told Him; however, the Man said that since he was victorious with God and man, his name was now *"Israel."* Then Jacob, now named

Israel realized that he had an encounter with God and was confident he could go home and reconcile with his brother.

In Summary, Jacob's faith in God, his obedience, and the positive name change to Israel ensured the continuation of God's promise to give the land of Israel to Abraham and his descendants. Since then, the Hebrew nation became known as the *Israelites*.

***

Another example of a positive name change was with Simon. Before he became a disciple of Jesus, his Natural gift of employment was as a fisherman. Jesus asked him to follow Him, and He would bless him with the Spiritual gift to become a "fisher of men." (to be discussed in a later chapter)

One day when Jesus was with His disciples, He asked them who they thought He really was. Only Simon answered Him by acknowledging that He was the Son of God. Jesus told him that only God could have given him that revelation; therefore, Jesus changed his name from Simon to *Peter*, meaning a *"strong rock."* Further, upon him, *this rock,* He would build his church of new converts.

Peter, however, was an unpredictable man who rapidly changed back and forth from faith to doubt. For example, when the disciples were in a boat in the ocean, a violent storm occurred. Peter and the disciples saw Jesus' walking towards them on the water. Excitably, Peter asked Jesus if he could come out of the boat to meet Him, and He said, "come." By faith, Peter walked on water, too; however, as he approached Jesus, he stopped looking at Him and looked at the strong wind and waves around him. His faith wavered, and Peter immediately sank into the ocean! He screamed for Jesus to save him, and He did. Then Jesus asked Peter, since He was in the storm with him, why did he let his faith waver?

Too, Peter was quick-tempered, easily angered, and impulsive, especially when the Temple guards came to arrest Jesus. Peter believed he had to protect Jesus and quickly drew his sword and cut the ear off one of the guards! Jesus reprimanded Peter for his violent behavior, then healed the guard's ear.

Peter's quick temper flared again when the guards took Jesus to the Priest for questioning. Several people recognized him as one of

Jesus disciples; however, Peter cursed them and denied that he knew Jesus on three separate occasions!

After the third time, Jesus turned and looked at Peter, and he remembered that Jesus previously told him that he would deny Him three times by sunrise. Regretfully, Peter began weeping!

After Jesus' resurrection, He met with the disciples and restored Peter to his position as their leader and organizer of the new Christian converts.

Jesus knew beforehand that changing Simon's name to Peter would change his life. He became not just a fisherman but a "fisher of men," just as Jesus promised. However, by faith, Peter had to be obedient.

In Summary, although some of these people were inconsistent in their behavior, they were given several opportunities to use the spiritual gifts given to them. As a result, due to God's love, mercy and forgiveness, these ordinary people rose to the purpose of their new names, and each of them became the person God designed them to be.

Lastly, whether single or married, a name change represents a blessing.

Chapter Seven

"When the wicked rule, the people mourn."

Proverbs 29:2(b)

Names with Negative Results

The following four stories are examples of wicked leaders and men whom God punished. Their names were King Nebuchadnezzar, his son Belshazzar, Haman, an advisor to a king, and a disciple of Jesus named Judas Iscariot.

After a series of devastating events, one of these men eventually repented of his evil ways, but the others did not.

The first story is about King Nebuchadnezzar, an awful and cruel king of Babylon. He was wealthy, trusted only in himself and the power of his massive army. When he defeated the armies of different kingdoms, he took whatever was valuable or anything else he desired. He also ordered his army to kill or make slaves of their captives.

When the king defeated Jerusalem and Judah, he ordered his men to take the Sacred treasure out of King Solomon's temple and bring them back to Babylon to put into his temple.

Nebuchadnezzar, however, was an *idol worshipper* and ordered a *golden statue* erected for all in his kingdom to bow down anytime they heard his musicians playing. If anyone refused, their punishment was incineration in a fiery furnace.

One day, everyone bowed down except three Jewish slaves named Shadrach, Meshack, and Abednego. These men followed the Jewish Law that stated they were not to worship anything or anyone except their God.

The king was informed of their disobedience and ordered the men brought before him to question them. When asked why they didn't bow down to the statue, they answered that it was against their God's law to bow down to anything other than Him; therefore, they would never bow down to an idol. Further, if thrown into the fiery furnace were their punishment, then their God would save them if He so desired. But, if not, they still would never bow down to an idol.

Enraged at their answer, the king ordered the soldiers to make the fire seven times hotter, tie their hands, and throw them into the furnace!

The fire, however, was so hot until the soldiers immediately died!

The king watched the three men in the fire, expecting them to die; however, he saw a fourth man in the furnace with them. It confused and astonished him! All four of them were walking around, unbound and unharmed. He exclaimed that the fourth man's form looked like "the Son of (a) God."

The king ordered the men out of the furnace, but only three men came out. Neither their clothes burned, nor their hair singed, and the men did not smell like smoke. The king immediately pronounced death to anyone who said anything negative about the three Jewish men's God. Next, he ordered the men released and promoted them within his kingdom.

Even though Nebuchadnezzar had this experience with God, he was still unrepentant, selfish, and proud; therefore, God gave him a terrifying nightmare! He called for all his wise men to interpret the dream, but none could. So, angrily, the king ordered death for all the wise men.

Daniel, a respected Jewish slave, who was

a wise man also learned of the king's decree to kill all the wise men, including him. He asked to speak to the king. He requested extra time to interpret the anxious king's dream, and the king granted his request.

Later that night, God visited Daniel in a vision and told him what the dream meant. The next day, Daniel came before the king. Anxiously, the king asked Daniel if he could interpret his dream.

Daniel informed the king that his dream meant he would lose his kingdom, lose his mind and behave like an animal until he fully recognized that God was in control of everything, including the king. Daniel advised the king that he needed to repent, meaning to change his ways, or the dream would come true.

The king did not repent, and twelve months later, his nightmare came true! As he was walking on the roof of his palace, bragging and praising himself for his majesty, might, honor, and for building the great city of Babylon, suddenly, a Voice from heaven (God) proclaimed to the king that He was removing his authority from him. Further, God told the king that he had to leave the palace and live like an animal until he proclaimed that God was sovereign over everyone and everything!

Immediately, Nebuchadnezzar had a nervous breakdown! Just as the dream foretold, the king lived in the field eating grass like an animal. His hair grew like eagle's feathers, and his nails looked like claws.

However, after seven years, God had mercy toward Nebuchadnezzar and restored his mental health. Nebuchadnezzar looked towards heaven, blessed God, and admitted that he was wrong and that He was in control over everyone, everything, including him. Then God returned his kingdom to him.

***

The second story of a person with a negative name, but with a different ending, was a man named Belshazzar, Nebuchadnezzar's son and successor to his throne. As king, he was arrogant, selfish, boastful, prideful, and worshipped idol-gods. He did not honor nor respect God.

One day, Belshazzar held a feast and invited 1,000 noblemen, his wives, and his mistresses to drink from the gold and silver vessels stolen from

King Solomon's temple in Jerusalem. As they drank the wine, they praised the idol-gods of gold, silver, brass, iron, wood, and stone for their good fortune!

Suddenly, the fingers of a man's hand appeared on one of the walls, wrote four words, and the king was terrified! Not knowing what the words meant, the king screamed for his wise men to interpret the meaning, but none could!

The queen intervened and told the king about a servant named Daniel, who could interpret dreams just as he had for his father, Nebuchadnezzar. She believed Daniel could interpret the words, and the king summoned him.

Daniel came before the king, saw the writing, and advised him that the writing's interpretation was fatal! He reminded the king of his father, who God had richly blessed, but became prideful and lost his kingdom. However, unlike his father, who repented and apologized to God, the king continually dishonored God and praised himself! Lastly, Daniel informed the king that his kingdom would not last. That night, the Persian army attacked Babylon and killed King Belshazzar.

***

Another example of a person with a negative name was Haman, an incredibly **racist man**. He was an advisor and second in command to King Ahasuerus (Xerxes). The king ordered that when Haman appeared, the people in the kingdom were to bow in reverence to him.

One day, the king's servants told Haman that a Jew named Mordecai wouldn't bow down before him. Haman became enraged until he decided to kill Mordecai plus exterminate all Jews throughout the kingdom.

Deceitfully, Haman went to the king and claimed that some of the people in his kingdom were disobedient to the king's command. Haman asked the king to sign a decree to kill all *these people* for disobeying him. Haman secretly hoped the king would sign the order as he knew the signed law was irrevocable; however, it was a trick to kill Mordecai. The king agreed and hastily signed it.

However, the king nor Haman knew that the new queen, Queen Esther, was Jewish or Mordecai's niece. Not only was the queen beautiful, but she was the king's favorite new wife!

When Mordecai heard of the decree, he sent a message to Queen Esther about Haman's *racist* and *violent plans* to kill him, plus the *extermination* of all the Jews. Mordecai's message included that her purpose for being the king's new wife could mean that it was for *"such a time as this."*

Esther sent word back to Mordecai to advise all the Jews to fast and pray for three days, and then she would seek an audience with the king.

Queen Esther went to the king and requested that he and Haman come to a banquet she prepared especially for them. The king granted her request.

After the banquet, she asked the king again if he and Haman would attend another meal the next day. She promised she would reveal her real intention for preparing them such feasts, and the king happily agreed.

Haman went home and told his wife and friends that he believed he would receive another promotion since the king and queen invited him to dine with them for two consecutive days. Joyfully, Haman's family celebrated with him!

Haman's mind, however, was still on killing Mordecai! So, his family encouraged him to build a platform with a noose to hang Mordecai, then, on the next day, ask the king for permission to hang him.

The night of the second dinner, the king asked Queen Esther what she desired from him. The queen requested that her life and her people's lives be spared and not murdered! Enraged, the king asked who was trying to hurt her or her people?!

Queen Esther explained that Mordecai was her uncle, plus she too was Jewish, and Haman tricked him into signing an executive order to kill all Jews! The king was furious and left the room! He went to the palace garden to think of a solution as he knew his signed order to kill the Jews, including his wife, was irrevocable!

Once the angry king left the room, Haman was terrified! He rushed to where Queen Esther was sitting to beg for his life!

When the king returned and saw Haman sitting close to the Queen, he thought Haman was trying to molest her in his absence! Then he screamed for the guards to take Haman away, and they immediately removed him!

One of the king's servants advised him that

Haman had already built a platform to hang Mordecai; however, the angry king ordered the guards to hang Haman instead! The king signed a new and irrevocable order for the Jews to fight back for their lives!

Later, at the queen's request, the king ordered Haman's ten sons to be hung as well. The king then gave Mordecai Haman's possessions and position as second in command.

***

The fourth and final story is about a man named Judas Iscariot, one of the original twelve disciples of Jesus. Judas was also the treasurer of their group; however, he was stealing money from their treasury.

Initially, Judas gladly followed Jesus; however, when he realized Jesus was teaching about a Spiritual kingdom and not an earthly kingdom, he was upset! He thought Jesus' new kingdom meant that the Romans wouldn't rule over the Jews anymore!

Judas knew the Priests were jealous and angry toward Jesus because the people loved Him! They loved Jesus' compassion, His special gifts of teaching, healing, and His ability to accomplish many other miracles. Judas also knew the Priests feared losing their religious influence over the Jews and their Roman political positions.

The Priests conspired to find a way to arrest Jesus and take Him to the Chief Priest on fraudulent blasphemy charges. They knew that once He was found guilty, they could go to the Governor, Pontius Pilot, and demand that Jesus receive a death sentence. Only a Roman Governor could sentence anyone to death. The Priests, however, didn't know where Jesus was to arrest Him.

The Scripture states that Satan entered Judas, seducing him to see an opportunity to make some money. He went to the Sanhedrin Priests and told them that if they paid him, he would reveal where they could find Jesus. The Priests agreed and paid Judas 30 pieces of silver. Their signal was whomever Judas kissed was Jesus.

Later at dinner with His disciples, referred to as the Last Supper, Jesus revealed that one of them would betray Him. The disciples were shocked and confused; however, Jesus focused on Judas and said, "Do quickly."

That night, when the Priests found Jesus to arrest Him, as promised, Judas greeted Him by calling him "Rabbi" and kissed Him. Jesus looked at Judas and asked him if he was betraying him for a kiss? Then the Priest guards arrested Jesus!

After Jesus' arrest, Judas felt consumed with guilt for his betrayal of Jesus and his knowledge of Jesus' subsequent death. Judas tried to give the money back to the Priests, saying that he sinned and was responsible for causing innocent bloodshed. The Priest, however, refused to take the money! Now they could continue with their plans to have Jesus wrongly accused and be put to death.

Judas was very aware of the Jewish Law that stated, "Bloodshed defiles the land," and atonement cannot be made except by "the blood of him that shed it." Therefore, for his betrayal of Jesus, *Judas committed suicide*.

Today, to be called a Judas is equal to one who betrays and causes mental or physical harm to a friend.

***

In Summary, the Scripture states that some leaders, under Satan's influence, will *lie* on other people and say they are cursed due to their race, birthplace, skin color, or religious beliefs. But they are *actually racist* and relish dominion over others.

God, however, **cannot be a racist,** as the Scripture states that He created "*Man in His Image, male and female.*" When these leaders dishonor God and His Word, the Scripture states they are fools, full of pride, and arrogantly worship themselves.

Leaders and men like these examples deceive themselves, betray God, their Creator, their families, friends, and others. They actually miss the plan, purpose, and powerful gifts God intended to place within their names. Therefore, the mention of their names is always negative.

Chapter Eight

Most Negative Name Changes

The most *negative* name changes occurred after God created Lucifer, the most beautiful Angel in heaven. Lucifer was the other Angel's leader, and their responsibilities were to fulfill God's assignments.

Due to his beauty and position, Lucifer became vain, egotistical, self-absorbed, and envious of God's authority. He *thought* he could dethrone God, then take His place and rule heaven.

Lucifer also coerced one-third of the Angels to rebel with him, and they *thought* their rebellious line of thinking was not treasonous towards God either.

God knew of their unified thoughts; therefore, He immediately kicked Lucifer and those Angels out of heaven, forever!

Once permanently removed and banned from heaven, God *changed* Lucifer's name to Satan, the Devil, a liar, the father of lies, the serpent, a murderer, and the evil one. God also renamed the other Angel's devils, demons, and unclean spirits.

Jesus also confirmed that He saw Satan fall from heaven like lightning! (to be discussed in a later chapter)

Satan and the demon's goals were to influence Adam and Eve to commit treason against God too. Satan wanted to get them eternally dismissed from Gods' presence, like him and the other fallen Angels.

Satan entered a snake, then went into the Garden of Eden and spoke to Eve. He began misquoting, misleading, and lying to Eve about the fruit God commanded her and Adam not to eat. He told her *God intentionally made her imperfect,* and if she only ate the fruit, she would not die but would be perfect like God.

Eve *thought* the fruit looked good and ate it. Next, she gave the fruit to Adam, and instead of reminding her what God commanded, he ate some too.

When God found out they disobeyed Him, Adam and Eve's punishment was that they couldn't live forever or live in the Garden of Eden anymore. As a result, God permanently evicted them, then sent them into the wilderness to live and eventually die.

God told Satan that since he seduced Adam and Eve to disobey Him, there would always be a war between him and humanity, but he would fail. Then, on Judgment Day, God declared He would throw him into hell, the Lake of fire, *forever*!

Adam and Eve's allegiance then fell under Satan's dominion and evil desires. Since then, every person, born after that, *inherited* Adam and Eve's *rebellious nature (sin)* too. Satan's plan for humanity was for every person to commit treason by disobeying Gods' Word, then make a conscious or unconscious decision to be thrown into hell for eternity as well.

Fortunately, *Satan is only a spirit* and cannot create a body for himself; therefore, he must *seduce people* to use their bodies and do his evil work. He encourages these people to sabotage and be unfaithful in all relationships. Some examples are lying, disobedience to parents, the authorities, friendships, marriages, employers, co-workers, and church members, just to name a few.

Satan seduces parents to commit domestic violence against their spouses, children, and stepchildren. Others commit random acts of violence, such as assault, rape, and murder, regardless if the punishment is life in prison.

Satan also entraps world leaders to be egotistical, arrogant, narcissistic, and lord their positions over others. Sometimes, these leaders hate each other's political opponents and persuade their voters into hating them too.

Under Satan's influence, these leaders also hate people in their own country and other countries because of their nationality, skin color, or religious beliefs. Additionally, these leaders misuse other people's names to make them feel inferior and lose hope of a better future for themselves and their families.

Satan's *first goal*, however, is to stop anyone worldwide from hearing the gospel of Jesus Christ. He doesn't want us to know what our names mean to God. He distracts and deceives us into doing the opposite of God's will for our lives.

Secondly, if Satan cannot stop us from hearing the gospel, his *ultimate goal* is to ensure that our names are not in God's Book of Life. He doesn't want anyone accepting Jesus as their Savior because he doesn't want anyone to spend eternity in heaven where he was supposed to live.

Satan has other tools to use against us too. He wants us to *blame God* for our failures, which *we* intentionally committed. For example, *Adam blamed God* for creating his wife, Eve.

Satan also wants us to *blame others* for the failures in our lives. For example, *Eve blamed the snake* for seducing her into disobeying God.

Satan also tries to seduce us into *listening to other people's negative opinions* about ourselves. Any interference will cause us to miss Gods' unique design, purpose, and destiny if we give in to other's viewpoints. We, however, were born with a free will or the ability to make choices and do not have to obey Satan.

The Scripture states that Satan's other goals are threefold:

- First, to *Steal* (Your salvation, your gifts in your name, God's assignment and purpose for your life, through distraction, which God calls the lust of the eye).
- Second, to *Kill* (Your body before you can accept Jesus through disease, abuse, neglect, a fatal sex drive, drug and alcohol addiction, or murder, which God calls the lust of the flesh.)
- Third, to *Destroy* (Your Soul, which is

your *conscious mind, will and emotions, loss of empathy and love for anyone, and narcissism*, which God calls the pride of life).

Satan *uses his demons to distract* us from receiving our gifts through manipulation and misdirection by anyone, including church members. The demon's names, which are named the lust of the flesh, are:

- Adultery (sex, but not with your spouse).
- Fornication (sex, but not married to them).
- Uncleanness (foul, immoral, or spiritually impure ties).
- Lasciviousness (lustful, lewd desires).
- Idolatry (worships of idols, money, excessive attachment to things, or persons other than God).
- Witchcraft (sorcery, magic, or summoning unclean spirits).
- Hatred (prejudice, severe racism, intense dislike, ill will, or rejection of one's true self).
- Variance (disagreement, discord, dispute).
- Emulation (impersonation, imitate, copy).
- Wrath (vengeful, rage, uncontrolled anger.)

- Strife (friction, quarrel, struggle, contention for superiority, chaos with family, friends, other nationalities, politics, or religious denominations).
- Sedition (treason, mutiny, and resistance to lawful authority).
- Heresies (blasphemy, erroneous beliefs, omitting truth, lies, division, intentionally spreading disagreement, discord, and gossip among people, families, communities, and your church).
- Envy (resentment, uncontrolled jealousy of another person due to their race, sex, or good fortune).
- Murder (to kill with malice, premeditation, put an innocent person to death, assassination, or suicide).
- Drunkenness (intoxication or passionate rage of the mind through addictions, such as alcohol, drugs, sex, and many others).
- Revile (abusive language or words to another person, shame, disgrace, humiliation, and blaming others)

Too, Satan and his demons want each of us to *overestimate ourselves* to discredit others, especially if we have low self-esteem of our worth and abilities.

Sometimes, it's *just the opposite*, and we are defiant, arrogant, full of self-pride, and unwilling to follow God's plans for our lives.

Satan intentionally *pressures and distracts* many people until they are stressed out too. If he succeeds in distracting them from turning to God for answers, they will never get to know what their name means to God. Unfortunately, as previously mentioned, some of them will destroy themselves through destructive behavior.

Finally, Satan does *not want us to share our finances* either. He doesn't want us to give our extra money to charitable organizations that feed, house, and clothe the poor locally or worldwide. Jesus said, however, He would repay anyone who shares their good fortune with the poor.

In Summary, Satan and those demon's decisions negatively impacted their names and the direction of their eternal existence. Their goals are for all people to make a conscious choice to be disobedient to God and His Word and go to hell with them.

Chapter Nine

Something to Think About

I believe the following statements pertain to each of us. God created us in His unique image; however, I will use myself as an example.

I have a Spirit.

- My spirit is the living force within me that gives my body life, energy, movement, and power.
- My spirit is God's very own living breath within me, which makes me alive. Why? When *God blew His Spirit, His breath* into Adam, His powerful breath continued into Eve and every human born.

I have a Soul.

- My soul is my conscious mind, rationale, and immortal self; my thoughts, emotions; my personality; my free will or the ability to make choices; self-control or not, and the ability to develop social and intimate relationships, moral or immoral.

The war between God and Satan, for control over my soul, is fought in my mind. My mind determines where my soul will live throughout eternity. I choose whom I will listen to during my lifetime. Then with my free will, I decide to live forever with or without God.

I have a Body.

- It is my physical self, which houses my spirit and my soul.
- It demonstrates the results of words I say to myself, the thoughts I think about myself and others, and my actions or reactions, positive or negative, that I choose to have daily. People recognize my body by my name.

All three parts of me: Spirit, Soul, and Body, have distinct functions; however, the three of them are one person, me. In the Scripture, God said that He created me after Himself.

God is a Spirit.

- His unseen Holy Spirit spoke, and through His Word, His plans and organization for the universe became seen. Examples are the sun, moon, planets, earth, nature, animals, and humans. His Spirit controls all things, and His Spirit will never die.

God has a Soul

- He has thoughts, feelings, and emotions, such as love, joy, forgiveness, grief, and anger. His Soul is revealed and shared with each of us through the Scripture in the Bible.

God has a Body.

- God's *physical self came* into the world *named Jesus*. He demonstrated His original thoughts, words, and actions through the ministry of Jesus. He planned to show us how we, too, should allow Him to work in our bodies, through our gifts, as He did through the miracles of Jesus. No one can defeat God, so whatever platform He chooses for our lives, whether writing, teaching, athletics, as parents and other gifts, He is within us, using us to accomplish His goals.

All three parts of Him, Spirit, Soul, and Body, have distinct functions; however, the Scripture states that these *"three are One."*

Chapter Ten

God Introduced His Name:

Jehovah, 1st Name of the Godhead

In the Beginning God created the heavens and the earth. And the Spirit of God moved upon the face of the water...
Genesis 1:1, 2(c)

God the Spirit

Throughout the Scripture, it states that God is a Spirit. We cannot see His Spirit; however, we all can feel the evidence of Him, and most of us can see it. For example, we feel the wind, breathe in and exhale air, and see seasons change each year.

Gods' character, personality, and attributes of His unseen Spirit are named the *Fruit of the (His) Spirit*. They are:

- Love (admiration, devotion, affection)
- Joy (happiness, gladness, merriment)
- Peace (harmony, order, calm, tranquility)
- Long Suffering (endurance, patience, tolerance, waiting with confidence)
- Gentleness (compassion, gracious, tender, pleasant)
- Goodness (excellence, benevolence, virtue)

- Faithfulness (loyal, faithful, sincere, honest, trustworthy)
- Meekness (gentle, kind, forbearing, humane)
- Temperance (restraint or self-control, moderation)

Even though we can't see Him, God also wanted men to know His name(s). In the Scripture, He told:

- Abraham: I AM the Almighty God.

- Moses: I AM THAT I AM, and the Lord God of the Hebrews.

- Isaiah: I AM the First, and I AM the Last; and besides me, there is no God.

- Jeremiah: I AM the Lord, the God of all flesh.

- John: I Am Alpha and Omega, the Beginning and the End.

God, however, revealed to Moses that His proper name was "JEHOVAH."

The Scripture states that there are powerful, Spiritual, and honorable benefits in God's name too. For example, God is a Healer, Protector,

Savior, and many more.

Before our birth, the Spirit of God also placed these powerful Spiritual and honorable benefits, plus His personality, the Fruit of His Spirit, within our proper names too. These attributes are activated when one accepts Jesus as their Savior. We are then *Spiritually born again.* (to be discussed more in-depth in Chapter 14)

In the New Testament, the disciples asked Jesus, since God is a Spirit, what name should they pray to Him? Jesus said to honor Him and begin their prayers with "Our Father," as found in the Lord's Prayer. He is the Creator of all things, so then, He is Our Father.

In Summary, since God is a Spirit and we cannot see Him, the Spirit of God inspired men to write the Bible. Why? He wanted each of us to know Him personally; therefore, when we read the Scripture, it is as though we are looking into our *Father's eyes.*

Chapter Eleven

God Introduced His Name:

Jesus, 2nd Name of the Godhead

Wherefore God also hath highly exalted him and given him a name which is above every name, that at the name of Jesus every knee should bow.
  Philippians 2: 9, 10(a)

I've already discussed that God is a Spirit; He has a Soul and a Body. Now, I will begin with His Body.

God has a Body

In the Old Testament, a prophet named Isaiah prophesied that a child would be born to a virgin, and this child's name would be Emmanuel, meaning **God with us**. Additional names of the baby would be "*the Mighty God*, the *Everlasting Father*, and the *Prince of Peace.*"

In the New Testament, God revealed to the Apostle John that He planned to come to earth, *as Jesus*, before He created the heavens and the earth. In the Scripture, John wrote, "In the beginning was the Word, and the Word was with *God,* and the *Word was God."* *Jesus was* actually *the Word, the Mighty God,* and the *Everlasting Father,* who became human. John additionally wrote, "He was in the world, and the world was made by Him, and the world knew Him not." *Jesus* is also called the *Prince of Peace.*

God's purpose for coming to earth was in His earthly name, Jesus, meaning Savior, Deliverer, and Messiah. He wanted to redeem humanity, His children, from Satan's rule, back to Himself.

The *Mighty God came* to earth in a body, born *as a baby*, just like us, to live among us. He wanted us to know that He understood the life we experience from birth until our death. He demonstrated how we should live by faith in God every day and showed us how to fulfill God's purpose for our lives.

From His youth, Jesus was obedient to His earthly parents and the authorities. He also attended Synagogue, went to religious ceremonies, and studied the Scripture.

As an adult, Jesus' was employed as a carpenter, which was His Natural gift.

Then, at approximately 30 years old, He began His ministry.

His Spiritual gift was teaching the good news of salvation, which was Gods' Love, sacrifice, the forgiveness of sin, and eternal life.

Jesus was also tempted and seduced by Satan in the same way we get tempted; however, He didn't sin. God, as Jesus, would never sin or rebel against His own Word. The temptations of Jesus made His physical mind, soul, and body strong enough to endure false accusations and His ultimate crucifixion.

Further, during our temptations, Jesus provided believers with the same powerful mindset that He had. As God and the *Prince of Peace*, He demonstrated how we also have His Peace during our trials. As a bonus, the Scripture states that He does not allow any more trouble or heartache placed on us than we can tolerate. In reality, our temptations cause us to grow and mature like Jesus.

Of course, as believers, we still sin, but the Scripture states that we can quickly ask God for forgiveness, and we will immediately receive it. Additionally, He will forgive us of our sins and never remember them anymore. As proof, the Scripture states, "He will cast all of our sins into the depths of the sea." *We still, however, are responsible for the consequence of our actions.*

In the Old Testament, and before the birth of Jesus, God said, "Life is in the blood"; therefore, when Adam and Eve disobeyed God, He killed a young, pure, and unbred lamb to make amends for their sin. Later on, God commanded the Priests to sacrifice pure and unbred lambs to make amends for the sin of the Jews.

God, however, no longer desired the blood of animals any longer; therefore, through Jesus, He came to earth to be the *pure, unblemished lamb and the final blood sacrifice for all men.* His blood, one time like His breath, was so powerful that it paid the price for the forgiveness of all humanity's inherited sin, present sins, and future sins.

In Summary, we can clearly see how the body, the blood, and why the name of Jesus is essential. When anyone accepts the loving sacrifice of Jesus,

God sees the spotless blood of Jesus covering all the sins of those who have received Him.

God has a Soul

God's Soul is packed with thoughts and emotions that He wanted us to know about Him personally. So, in the Old Testament, God instructed Moses to tell the Hebrew nation that His Soul would be pleased with them if they were obedient to His instructions.

As Jesus, He displayed His soul, which is His thoughts and emotions. He experienced the same feelings as we do, such as:
- Crying (Jesus wept.)
- Fear (sweat blood, His crucifixion.)
- Anger (Priests accused Jesus of healing on the Sabbath day instead of seeing His Divinity at work, beating merchants out of the Temple for selling religious items for profit only.)
- Sorrow/Anguish ("sorrowful" in the Garden of Gethsemane.)
- Humility (obeying Gods' purpose for Him.)
- Compassion (healing the sick, driving out mentally or violently ill demons in people

and raising the dead back to life.)
- Hunger and Thirst (after fasting 40 days and nights; thirsty while hanging on the cross.)
- Love (for His mother, dying for humanity.)

As Jesus, He demonstrated how to have an abundant life by exhibiting His social skills as well. For example:
- He regularly attended synagogues (church), religious celebrations, and weddings with His family and friends.
- He had dinner with people of various social statuses, such as fraudulent tax collectors, the poor and disenfranchised, and those with mental and moral issues.
- He loved children, and they loved Him too. They eagerly listened to and followed Him.

Jesus told the adults that if they wanted to follow Him, they had to have a childlike perspective as well.

In Summary, God came to earth as Jesus to redeem His children, and since He is the Creator of all things, He *never fails* to accomplish his goals. Therefore, this is why His human name, Jesus, is the name above all names. *He is a loving God in human form.*

Chapter Twelve

God Introduced His Name:

The Holy Spirit, 3rd Name of the Godhead

*For there are three that bear record in heaven,
the Father, the Word, and the Holy Ghost;
and these three are one.*
1st John 5:7

After John baptized Jesus, the powerful Holy Spirit descended from heaven and entered Him. Jesus' baptism confirmed His willingness to accept His earthly gifts, ministry, and Spiritual purpose. God, the Father in heaven, spoke, affirming that Jesus was His son and He was "well pleased" with Him.

The Holy Spirit then led Jesus into the wilderness to be tempted by Satan, but first, Jesus fasted, without food, for forty days and nights. At the end of His fasting, Satan immediately appeared to tempt and seduce Jesus into serving him.

Satan knew Jesus was weak from hunger. He suggested that if Jesus was the Son of God, He should make bread from the rocks to feed Himself, just as he successfully defeated Adam, Eve, and Esau with food. The Holy Spirit spoke, through Jesus, reminding Satan of the powerful words of the Scripture, which states, "It is written that man shall not live by bread alone but *by every Word of God.*"

Next, Satan suggested Jesus should leap from the highest point of a temple, hoping He would commit suicide. This time, Satan *lied* by *misquoting* the Scripture, saying that the Angels would catch Him. But, again, the Holy Spirit, within Jesus, correctly said, "Thou shalt not tempt the Lord *thy* God."

Finally, Satan promised Jesus that if He turned away from God and worshipped him, he would give him worldly fame, riches, and prestige. Again, the Holy Spirit, within Jesus, reminded Satan of the Scripture, which states, "It is written, thou shall worship the Lord *thy* God, and Him only *shall thou serve.*" Defeated, Satan left.

Satan clearly did not recognize that God, the Holy Spirit, within Jesus, spoke directly to him. Additionally, Satan did not consider that the Holy Spirit led Jesus into the wilderness to personally defeat him again, but this time, on earth. In the Scripture Jesus said, "I and my Father are One."

Satan thought he could simply tempt and seduce Jesus, the man, in disobeying God. Jesus, however, could not obey Satan, as Jesus *is* God.

For humanity, sometimes our temptations are like our spirit, soul, and body *are on fire*, much like the three Hebrew men's story in the fiery furnace. We must remember that a fourth man was in the fire with them and our comforter, the Holy Spirit, is with us through any extreme temptation as well. We defeat Satan's alluring seductions and deceitful lies by remembering God's Word, both in the Natural and Spiritual realm of our lives.

This scenario also demonstrated how to stay focused on God's purpose and plans for us, despite the temptation's turbulence. For example, the Apostle Peter boldly "walked on water" in the storm to meet Jesus; however, he sank when he took his eyes off Him. Peter then cried for Jesus to rescue him. When our faith wavers in our storms, if we cry out to Him, His Holy Spirit will save us too. The Scripture states that He will provide a way for us to escape any temptation.

The Holy Spirit doesn't want us to be distracted by temptations or lusts for egotistical desires either, such as *obsessing* over having a lot of money, possessions or controlling other people. Instead, we are to stay focused on following His purpose for us.

After His temptations, the Holy Spirit gave Jesus the power to perform His mission on earth, which included performing many miracles. For example, Jesus cast demonic spirits out of the mentally ill, healed the disabled, those with debilitating diseases, fed thousands with a small amount of food, and raised the dead back to life.

Before Jesus completed His earthly mission, He promised His disciples that He would not leave them alone or without someone to comfort them when He left. Instead, He said He would send a Comforter to take His place, or the Holy Spirit, that was within Him. The other name of the Comforter was the Spirit of Truth, or *God Himself*, Who would come and reside *within* each of them.

Next, strangely enough, He said, *"I will come to you."* Then, He said the Father and I would come and live within each believer.

When Jesus rose from the dead, His first action was breathing on the disciples saying, *"Receive ye the Holy Ghost."* It was like God blowing His breath into Adam, making him physically alive, and God, through Jesus, breathing on them to make them *Spiritually alive or born again. His breath* prepared the disciples for the Holy Spirit's infilling and to receive their gifts.

Before His ascent into heaven, Jesus told His disciples and other believers to remain in Jerusalem and wait for the Holy Spirit to return. Obediently, they followed His instructions.

After several days of praying, the Holy Spirit entered each person. They immediately began praising and worshiping God in various unknown languages, which they had never spoken. Their worship was the confirmation that the gift and power of the Holy Spirit were within each one, just like Jesus said would happen. The Holy Spirit gave each of them powerful gifts to go everywhere and tell others the good news that salvation and restoration to God were through Jesus.

The gifts the Holy Spirit gave them were organizational and administrative skills, wisdom, insight, faith, prophesying, preaching, teaching, healing, encouraging others, giving finances, and many more. The Holy Spirit still gives these powerful gifts to each believer today.

No gift, however, big or small, is more important than any other believer's gift, even if our names or skills are the same. We are not to compete with each other but lovingly function together, as one body, as the Holy Spirit designed.

On earth, *we are* the total body of Jesus. Some are His hands, feet, eyes, and other parts of His body, but we are one, like Jesus, the complete Image of God.

The Scripture states that God orders the steps of a good man; therefore, we cannot really fail. The Scripture also says, "For though a righteous man may fall seven times, he still gets up." God's mercy will always allow us to begin again. Lastly, *God* is actually doing the work through us; therefore, He *cannot be defeated.*

No one is too young or too old to begin a relationship with His Holy Spirit. Jesus stated that He would never reject us or leave us but would be within us and guide us throughout our lifetime.

In Summary, God is the Father in Creation; He is the Son, Jesus in Salvation, and He is the gift-giving Holy Spirit within us. Therefore, as the Scripture states, *these three are One.*

Chapter Thirteen

Final Evidence

The Scripture tells a story about a Master going on a long trip. He called three of his servants to run His affairs while He was gone.

Before He left, He gave one servant five pieces of money, to another servant two pieces and another servant, one piece, *each according to their ability and understanding.*

Once the Master left, the servant's given five and two pieces of money doubled their money; however, the servant He gave one piece of money, dug a hole in the ground, buried it, and went on about his business.

When the Master returned home, He was pleased to learn two of His servants doubled His money. As a reward, He gave them more of His property to manage.

However, the servant with the one piece of money handed it back to Him. But first, he blamed his Master for not increasing His money. The servant told Him that He was a harsh man and expected a return on something He didn't earn.

Secondly, the servant said that he was afraid of Him; therefore, he buried the money to give back to Him when He returned home.

The Master was outraged and told the servant that He trusted him with an opportunity to increase the treasure freely given to him! Further, if he knew He was such a harsh man, why didn't he put the money in the bank to earn interest for Him!

This servant's behavior openly displayed that he did not honor nor respect his Master. The Master *named* him *"wicked and slothful" for his attitude and irresponsible behavior.* Then, He threw him out of His house forever! The Master blessed the servant, who doubled his five pieces, with the wicked servant's money.

First, this story is an example of people who refuse to accept the gift of God's Son, Jesus, during their lifetime. Instead, they lie, disrespect, and blame God for their inaction, which is an example of burying their gift. They also are named "wicked and slothful." The Scripture states that when they die, they too will be forever banished from God's presence!

Secondly, this story is also an example of how

God offers His Holy Spirit, a priceless treasure, through Jesus. Once a person accepts His gift of Jesus, His Holy Spirit will reveal the true treasures He placed in their names.

In reality, God cannot reward anyone who mismanages the gift and purpose that He had for their lives. They will never come into the knowledge that it is really God, the Holy Spirit, actually doing the work through them. Instead, they selfishly and *erroneously think* that it's "their right" to do as they please and still receive a reward from God.

Once a person starts with the minimum gift and multiplies the talent given, His Holy Spirit will provide additional gifts and skills to multiply and operate in their local church, plus the corporate church. In return, God only asks that we introduce others to Jesus so they, too, will find out the gifts in their names.

Lastly, disobedience to Gods' will is like disobeying the first commandment given to Adam and Eve, which was to "be fruitful and multiply." Since we are born in His Image, we too are to imitate God, our Father, and multiply the gifts

He gave us. The Scripture states that rebellion or failure to obey His instructions is like practicing the sin of witchcraft.

In Summary, these stories of disobedience, like the "wicked and slothful servant," Satan plus one-third of the Angels, Adam, Eve, and Cain, demonstrate how *each of them overestimated themselves* and *underestimated God.* They *believed their thoughts* or *someone else's opin*ion was *correct* for their lives instead of Gods' instructions.

They all bore the same eternal punishment. For example, one-third of the Angels were kicked out of heaven and sentenced to hell forever! Adam and Eve were expelled from the Garden of Eden forever! God dismissed Cain from His presence forever, and the "wicked and slothful servant" was thrown out of Masters' home permanently!

Chapter Fourteen

How Do I Find Out What My Name Means?

First, this book is not a formula or scheme. It's about having a *quiet, one-on-one relationship* with God through Jesus and discovering why we were born.

Secondly, it's about how we are *to listen* to Him, through His Holy Spirit, as He explains His purpose for our lives, both Naturally and Spiritually. We listen to Him by reading the Scripture and meditating on His Word.

Third, through His Holy Spirit, He will reveal how to successfully *follow* His leading in the Natural and Spiritual realms and work through us, whether we are teenagers, parents, writers, musicians, athletes, teachers, seniors, and many more.

In the Natural Realm, each of us is encouraged to pursue a good education and not associate with those who are disobedient and have evil intentions. God *commanded that we work,* and as parents or caretakers, we are the first to model such goals.

We should also inspire others to follow God's purpose for their lives. There are many examples of people who followed Gods' plan for their lives and used their successful platforms to inspire others. For example:

- Entertainers, Actors
- Athletes, Coaches
- Medical Personnel, Doctors and Nurses
- Teachers and Professors
- Politicians,
- Community activists, and many more.

In the Spiritual Realm, God wants each of us to use our gifts to bring others into the knowledge of who He is. There are many benefits to our obedience. For example, in the Old Testament, by faith:

- Noah obeyed God and built an Ark before the great flood to save the human race. Because of his obedience, we exist today.

- Abraham, although childless, agreed and moved away from his relatives' influence. At 100 years old, God blessed him with a child and, later, many descendants. Abraham believed God and followed His instructions; therefore, Abraham is the *Father of Faith*. God also commanded us to live our lives by faith.

- Moses obeyed God and led the Hebrews, Abraham's descendants, out of slavery from Egyptian captivity. Then, God gave him the Ten Commandments to provide to His people to live by, and the commandments are for us today.

- Joshua, Moses' successor, obeyed God and successfully led the Hebrews into the land God promised Abraham. Their descendants were later named Israelites, and they exist today.

In the New Testament, by faith:

- A disciple named Peter obeyed Jesus and preached to the Jews that Jesus was indeed the Messiah. Therefore, Peter became the new Christian converts leader, and we exist today.

- The Apostle Paul obeyed Jesus and taught the Gentiles/non-Jews about Him.

Paul authored many books instructing new believers about the teachings of Jesus and how Jesus wanted every believer to live. Today, his books are in the New Testament of the Bible.

Tithing

In the Natural Realm, God has another benefit. It is a mathematical system called tithing. Tithing is giving 10% of *your gross income* to your local church. God promises to provide multiple blessing's when you willingly give your tithes.

The book of Genesis explains how tithing began. Abram, later known as Abraham, had a nephew named Lot, who was taken captive during the war of kings. Abram took hundreds of his servants and successfully defeated the king who captured him.

Abram and Lot were victoriously returning home when they met a Priest of God named Melchizedek. The Priest blessed Abram and said, "Blessed be Abram of the most high God, possessor of heaven and earth, which hath delivered thine enemies into thy hand."

To *thank God* for his victory in recovering his nephew, Abram blessed the Priest with 10% of all the treasure he acquired from the battle.

Later in a vision, God appeared to Abram and told him that He would be his protector for *honoring Him in his giving*. Tithing, however, was not mandatory at that time.

Eventually, tithing became law for Abraham's descendants as God *commanded them* to tithe 10% from their crops, flocks, and money to give to the Priest's to sustain them. The Priest's did not work; therefore, with the tithe, the Priest's fed their families, the widows, orphans, strangers, and used some money for their temple's upkeep. The Priests, in turn, continually prayed and offered sacrifices to God on behalf of the people's sins.

The people, however, became disobedient and stopped giving their tithes and offerings. Through a prophet named Malachi, God told His people that they were robbing him, and He will punish them for their disobedience.

God, however, promised if they returned to tithing, He would no longer be angry with them. He said to test Him and see if He would again pour out His blessings upon them. He assured them that they would not have enough room to contain it all.

When giving a 10% tithe to your local church, it helps to support your Pastor, who ministers to your congregation, pay church bills, provide programs to help those in need in your community, and support specific missionaries around the world. Except for taxes, the rest of your money belongs to you.

The blessing of tithing is that you can still manage and support your family's needs, including savings, household expenses, transportation, and entertainment. You also can establish an emergency fund, a college fund for your children, and a retirement fund for yourself.

Many people come to faith in Jesus because of your faithful giving. The Scripture states that all God asks is when you promise to give, do not break your promise, and not pay it.

In the New Testament, Jesus confirmed the tithing principle, but He admonished the public officials and church leaders for being hypocrites. He told them that yes, they tithe, but they showed a false appearance of virtue or religion because they left out (good) judgment or turned a blind eye to wrongdoing, mercy, and faithfulness.

Just as Jesus admonished them, *we should not*

be hypocrites when we tithe by leaving out (good) judgment, mercy, and faithfulness in our home, church, or community.

If, however, you cannot tithe 10% due to your current financial situation, make an agreement with God that you will start tithing with 1% of your gross earnings until you can give 10%. For example, Jesus was observing the wealthy giving a substantial offering at their Synagogue; however, a poor widow placed only two coins in the offering from what little money she had. So then, Jesus told his disciples that the wealthy gave a large donation from their surplus, but she gave the most significant offering.

Lastly, make sure you don't cheat God by adding any additional or unnecessary bills before you get to the point of giving 10%. The Scripture states that money will show where your heart stands with God. Either you will spend your money lavishly on yourself, like the selfish rich man's story, or as God designed.

In reality, all things, including your money, belongs to God. An example is when we die, we cannot take our money with us. Therefore, use your money as God commanded and be a blessing to your church so that your giving will bless others. In turn, God will protect and greatly honor you.

Spiritual Order of Tithing

In the Spiritual Order, just like a tithe, God has a powerful way to simplify your private time with Him.

Jesus, for example, asked Peter and two other disciples to accompany Him while He prayed; however, when He returned from praying, He found them asleep. He awakened Peter and asked him if he could not stay awake with Him for "one hour?"

His Holy Spirit also asks each of us can we spend an hour a day with Him too? In an hour, we can develop an excellent and personal relationship with Him in worship. Examples are thanking Him for Jesus saving us, singing Him a song, thanking Him for choosing us to assist Him in both the Natural and Spiritual realms or reading a chapter from the Bible. We can also discuss our family or work concerns with Him.

As a result of worship, studying, and meditating on the Scripture, we spend time with Him.

If we don't have a solid hour in our schedule, break an hour into increments of ten or twenty minutes each.

Gradually you will sense an awareness of what your name means to God and what He intends for you to accomplish, both Naturally and Spiritually.

In the Natural realm, for example, He may lead you to begin a business with your name, your initials, or give you an idea or title for a business.

In the Spiritual realm, God selects many people to preach; however, each preacher has a distinctive style and will reach a different audience. It's the same with other platforms. We will have a different audience to reach as well.

Knowing who *you are* and *your purpose* in life has a lifelong effect on you, your family, friends, and community.

Lastly, His Holy Spirit will also direct you where you belong in your local church. However, He wants you to remember, *your service to Him is to reclaim His children back to Him.* Therefore, allow His Holy Spirit to use your gift(s) and platform to fulfill His goals.

In Summary, I cannot tell or promise you that I know the answer to what your name means to God; however, I know that in the Scripture, God said, "Call unto Me, and I will answer thee, and shew thee great and mighty things, which thou knowest not."

How precious also are thy thoughts unto me, O God!
How great is the sum of them!
Psalms 139:15

Chapter Fifteen

Conclusion

At the beginning of time, God set the blueprint for naming and told us His name was God, our Creator. Later, to Moses, He said His proper name was Jehovah. The Scripture states that God's name is to be honored, and since He created us in His Image, our names are honorable as well. We are His children, and what the Father has, we have it too.

God named the first man Adam. He did not want Adam to be alone, so He created a helper for him. Adam named her Woman; however, since God created her from one of Adam's ribs from within his body, God called them both Adam.

Moreover, God gave them both a Natural and Spiritual Order which I call *special gifts*. The first Natural Order given was the commandment to work. God told Adam to name all the animals He created and take care of the Garden of Eden where he lived. Once the woman was created, she was to assist him in his duties. This commandment for employment continues for all of us today.

The first Spiritual Order given to them was to have a daily relationship with God, multiply themselves by having children, and naming them. The rest of humanity was to follow God's pattern as well.

God additionally placed *special gifts* in our names like Himself. For example, in the name of Jesus, His gifts included Savior, Healer, Teacher, and Emmanuel, meaning God with us, just to name a few. So likewise, your gift may be a leader, a giver, a teacher, a doctor, and other gifts like Him.

He commanded that we must learn as much as possible about these gifts through education, training, and practice for whatever special gifts He gives us.

We can best share our giftings wherever His Holy Spirit leads us. As we've learned, He uses our gifts as *spiritual platforms* to reclaim His children back to Him and out of Satan's dominance over us.

God gave us Natural and Spiritual gifts also to have fun and enjoy life as Jesus did. There are numerous ways to be social and have fun with our families, friends, and church members.

God also wants us to share our financial blessings by willing to give tithes and offerings to the local church where we attend. Tithing helps the Pastors and Priests to conduct their duties within the church and the community. Tithing also ensures that God will bless us in every area of our lives, like employment, family, finances, and good health.

Lastly, as I previously discussed, Satan hates God so much until he comes immediately to *confuse and distract* us from accepting Jesus as our Lord and receiving our gifts. He does not want any of us to listen or follow God's Word in the Bible, our Manual, to live our lives and operate our gifts successfully.

Satan, however, is only a spirit; therefore, he needs people to further and accomplish his goals of hate. *This Spirit of Hate is always his method.* He uses his demons to seduce people to distract us from accepting Jesus and the great gifts His Holy Spirit has for us. Satan really wants our allegiance to him and not to God.

A common term for people who succumb to Satan's influence is called "Haters;" however, *it is really Satan distracting them from their own purpose.* Some examples of his demonic influences are gossip, lies, cheating, racism, and murder.

Now, let's discuss *the keys* to find out what your name means to God. First, you must:

1.) Ask Jesus to come into your life as your Lord and Savior and forgive you of your inherited rebellious nature (sin) and your personal sins. As you have already read, Jesus will always forgive you as He *is* God in human form.

Jesus said, "*I am the Way*, the Truth, and the Life," and "*No man comes to the Father but by Me.*"

It's so easy to accomplish because all you must do is ask Him to come into your life, whether you're at home, watching a religious program, at church, in jail/prison, or on your deathbed. It is never too late, nor are you too young or old to receive Jesus into your life. *He is a loving God and will always welcome you.*

When God sees a believer, He will see the pure and sacrificial blood of Jesus covering you and ***cleansed from the deadly blood poisoning of disobedience,*** each of us inherited from Adam and Eve. Jesus also promised that no one could ever take you out of His hand.

2.) Attend a local church.

The Scripture states that we should "Not forsake the assembling of ourselves together" as we strengthen one another through fellowship and community worship.

3.) Tithe.

Many Scriptures promise to bless you for giving in your lifetime and to your descendants. Abraham and his descendants were blessed when they were obedient in giving their tithes. The Scriptures states, "For where your treasure is, there will be your heart also."

4.) Read the Bible; Attend Bible Study.

To personally know God is to read His Word and attend bible study so that you won't be embarrassed when interpreting the Scripture for yourself, your family, believers, or unbelievers.

5.) Prayer.

Your faithfulness in daily one-hour communication with God is one of the most important keys. The Scripture states, "Pray without ceasing," meaning always have open communication with God, especially during our temptations. However, once you pray, in return, you must *quietly listen* to hear from Him too.

Finally, as previously stated, just like the Master gave each of his servants something valuable to manage, the Scripture says that when God returns, through Jesus, **He will call each one of us, by name,** *to give an account* for our lives. He will ask you:
- Did you ask Jesus to come into your heart so that your name is in My Book of Life?
- Did you multiply your Natural and Spiritual gifts given to you, or did you bury them?
- Did you submit your body to Me, like Jesus, so that I could use your gifts to accomplish My goals?
- Did you spend an hour with Me every day?
- Did other's opinions influence you in your life's purpose and not Me?
- Did you use My Word for your own selfish, vain and egotistical agenda, like money or fame, both Naturally and in Ministry?

In Conclusion, God told us His name, the gifts in His name, and our names so we can assist Him in reclaiming his children. Therefore, I firmly believe *Your Gift from God is in Your Name.*

Scriptures for the Introduction

Psalm 127:3-5(a)

Psalm 139:15-18; Jeremiah 29:11; John 3:16

John 10:10(b)

Proverbs 1:7; 3:13-26; Proverbs 4:5-9,12-13

1Corinthians 12:1, 4-14, 18, 25, 27-28

Genesis 1: 26(a), 27-28; Psalm 100:3

Genesis 2:8, 15, 19-20(a); Genesis 2:18, 20(b), 21

Genesis 2:16-17

Genesis 3:8-11; 23-24

Revelation 20:12-13

Scriptures for Chapter One

1 Samuel 16:11-13(a)(b); Acts 13:22

1 Samuel 17:34-37(a)

2 Samuel 6:12(b), 14-15, 18-19

2 Samuel 5:4

1 Chronicles 29:26-28(a)

***

I Chronicles 29:22(b)-25, 28(b)

I Kings 3:5-14; 2 Chronicles 1:1, 7-12

Proverbs 29:2(a)

***

Luke 16:19-26

Matthew 25:34-40; Luke 6:38; Luke 14:13-14

Scriptures for Chapter Two

Genesis 4:1-2(a)

Genesis 1:14

Genesis 4:2(b)(c)

Hebrews 9:27(a)

I Corinthians 12:1, 4-12, 28

Hebrews 9:27(b)

Deuteronomy 6:5

Exodus 20:3-17; Deuteronomy 4:6-14, 16-21

Leviticus 19:17-18(b); Matthew 7:12; Luke 10:27-28

Scriptures for Chapter Three

Genesis 2:7(b)(c), 19(b), 20(b), 22-23, 24(b)(c)-25

Genesis 2:16-17

Genesis 3:6-7, 23-24

Genesis 3:20

Genesis 4:1-2

Genesis 3:21

Genesis 4:3-12; Genesis 3:21; Leviticus 17:11(a)

Genesis 4:25

Scriptures for Chapter Four

Genesis 12:1-4; Genesis 17:5; Romans 4:3,16(a)-21

Exodus 12:40; Acts 7:6

***

Exodus 3:1, 4(b), 7, 10

Exodus 12:1-31; Exodus 20:1-17, 23

***

Joshua 1:1-9; Joshua 21:43-45; Joshua 23:1; Joshua 24:29

***

Isaiah 7:14; Isaiah 53:2-12

***

Luke 1:26-35, 37-38; Genesis 1:2(c)-3

***

Matthew 1:18-21, 24-25; Matthew 13:55

***

Matthew 6:9-13; Luke 1:1-4

Genesis 1:1

Revelation 2:17

Scriptures for Chapter Five

Luke 1:5, 7, 11-17, 24, 36, 39-41, 44, 57-58, 60, 63, 66(b)-67

Matthew 3:1-6, 11; Luke 3:2-4, 16

***

Luke 2:21, 40-49, 51-52

John 2:19, 21; Hebrews 10:4-5, 9, 12; Galatians 3:26-28

Matthew 3:13-17; 2 Corinthians 5:21

John 12:47

John 3:1-6, 17

Matthew 5:1-48

Matthew 4:23-24; Matthew 8:1-3, 5-10, 13-17; Matthew 13:54-58

Matthew 28:1-2, 5-7; Romans 6:9, 14; Romans 8:11; Revelation 1:18

Revelation 20:10, 15

***

Acts 2:14-33, 36, 41; Acts 4:4

Mark 14:1; Mark 15:13

Acts 10:9-16; Acts 11:5-10

Acts 10:1-8

Scriptures for Chapter Five (cont.)

Acts 10:21-22, 34-48

***

Acts 8:3, Acts 26:5

Acts 9:1-6; Acts 26:15-18

Acts 9:10-25

Acts 13:9(a)

Acts 13:14, 42-44, 47-49

Romans 10:9-13; Titus 2:11

Ephesians 2:8-9; Matthew 19:17

2 Corinthians 11:23(b)-27

***

Genesis 3:23-24

John 10:7, 9, 10(b), 11; 1 Peter 2:24-25

John 3:3, 5-6

1 Corinthians 12:1, 4-14, 25, 28

Proverbs 24:16(a)

Scriptures for Chapter Six

Genesis 12:1-4

Genesis 17:1-8, 15-19

Genesis 21:1-3, 5-7; Galatians 3:6-9

***

Genesis 24:67; Genesis 25:20-23

Genesis 25:25-28; Genesis 25:29-34

Genesis 27:1-46; Genesis 28:1-7

Genesis 31:3; Genesis 32:7-8, 23-28; Genesis 33:4

***

Matthew 4:18-20; Matthew 16:13-19

Matthew 14:24-31; John 18:10-11

Matthew 26:69-74(a); Luke 22:61-62

John 21:14-17; Acts 2:36-38, 41,47

Scriptures for Chapter Seven

Proverbs 29:2(b)

2 Kings 24:10-11; 13; 2 Kings 25:11-12; 2 Chronicles 36:7

Daniel 3:1-6, 8-9, 12-30

Daniel 4:4-8, 24-37

***

Daniel 5:1-13, 18-30

***

Esther 2:2-20

Esther 3:1-6, 8-11

Esther 4:1-5, 9-10, 13-17

Esther 5:1-14; Esther 7:1-10

Esther 8:11; Esther 9:13-14, Esther 10:1-3

***

John 12:4-6

Matthew 26:3-5, Luke 22: 3

Matthew 26:14-16, 21, 24-25, 47-50

Matthew 27:3-5; Numbers 35:33

***

Genesis 1:26-27

Psalm 10:1; Psalm 14:1; Proverbs; 8:13

Scriptures for Chapter Eight

Isaiah 14:12-15; Ezekiel 28:13-17; Revelation 12:4, 9-10

Revelation 20:2; Revelation 16:14; Jude 1:6

Luke 10:18

Genesis 3:1, 4-6, 23-24; Genesis 3:14-15

Genesis 3:11

Romans 5:12, 19

Genesis 3:12-13

John 10:10 (a)

Galatians 5:19-21

1 Samuel 18:12; 1 Samuel 22:8; Matthew 2:3

1 Kings 16:30, 33; 1 Kings 19:1-21; 1 Kings 21:5-14

Matthew 25-40

Revelation 20:12-15

Scriptures for Chapter Nine

Genesis 1:2(c); Genesis 1:27; Isaiah 42:5(c); John 4:24

Leviticus 4:2; Acts 3:23; Romans 12:3; Philippians 4:8

Romans 12:1; 1 Corinthians 6:19

***

Genesis 1:1-2(c); 2 Samuel 23:2(a); Acts 2:17-18

Leviticus 26:11(b); John 3:16; John 11:35

Isaiah 7:14; John 1:1-3, 10, 14; 1 Timothy 3:16(b)

I John 5:7

Scriptures for Chapter Ten

Genesis 1:1-2; John 4:24; 2 Corinthians 3:17(a)

Genesis 1:3, 9-11, 14; Acts 2:2

Galatians 5:22-23

Genesis 17:1

Exodus 6:3

Jeremiah 32:27(a)

Isaiah 44:6

1 Corinthians 12:3-14

John 3:3, 6; Romans 10:9

Matthew 6:9-13

Mark 14:36(a); Romans 8:15; Galatians 4:6

Genesis 1:1, 2(c); John 1:1

2 Timothy 3:16

Scriptures for Chapter Eleven

Isaiah 7:14; Isaiah 9:6; Matthew 1:21-23

John 1:1-4, 10-14; John 10:10(b)

Hebrews 2:16-17; Hebrews 10:5

Isaiah 61:1-2; John 3:17-18(a); Philippians 2:9-11; Matthew 8:17

Luke 2:40-48, 51

Luke 3:23

John 3:16

Hebrews 4:15; 1 John 1:8-9; 1 John 2:1

Micah 7:18-19; I Corinthians 10:13

Romans 5:1-5; Romans 8:1, 37-39

Leviticus 17:11; Hebrews 10:3-4,10-12, 14

***

Leviticus 26:11; Jeremiah 32;41

John 11:35; Luke 22:42-44; Matthew 21:12-13; Mark 3:5

John 12:27

John 3:16; Philippians 2:8 Hebrews 10:7

Mark 5:25-26; John 11:1, 11, 14, 43-44

Luke 8:27-30, 35, 49-50, 54-55

Philippians 2:7-11

Scriptures for Chapter Eleven (cont.)

Matthew 9:22; Mark 5:8, 13, 34

Matthew 4:2; Matthew 21:18; John 19:28

John 19:25-27

John 10:10 (b); Matthew 4:13-16; Luke 4:16; John 2:1-2

Matthew 9:10; Mark 2:13-16

Matthew 18:2-6, 10

Matthew 19:13-15; Luke 18:15-17

John 10:28-30

Romans 14:11

John 1:1-4

Scriptures for Chapter Twelve

Luke 3:21-22

Luke 4:1-12; John 10:30

Daniel 3:21-25; Matthew 14:28-29; 1Corinthians 10:13-14

Matthew 8:28-35; Mark 5:1-17

John 4:46-54; John 9:1-7

Matthew 14:17-21; Matthew 27:50-54; Luke 7:11-17

John 14:16, 18, 23, 26

John 20:22

Acts 1:4-5, 8; Acts 2:1-4

I Corinthians 12:1, 4-14, 22, 25, 28

John 13:34-35; 1 Corinthians 12:13-27

Psalm 37:23-24; Proverbs 24:16

John 10:28-30

I John 5:7-8

Scriptures for Chapter Thirteen

Matthew 25:14-30; Luke 19:12-26

1 John 1:6, 8, 10; 1 John 4:7-8, 20; 1 John 5:10

John 20:22; Acts 1:8(a); 1 Corinthians 12:1, 3-11

1 Thessalonians 4:8; 1 Thessalonians 5:19; Romans 12:3

Acts 1:8(b); Hebrews 2:4

Matthew 24:14(a); Mark 13:10; Acts 1:8(b); Luke 24:47

Genesis 1:27-28(a); 1Samuel 15:23

Isaiah 14:13-14

Genesis 2:3, 6

Genesis 3:1; Genesis 3:11

Proverbs 16:18

Isaiah 14:12; Revelation 20:10

Genesis 3:23-24; Genesis 4:11-12(b)

Matthew 25:30

Scriptures for Chapter Fourteen

Psalm 22:9; Proverbs 1:5; Proverbs 1:7-8(a); Proverbs 4:7

John 16:13

Exodus 20:9; Proverbs 4:14-17

Genesis 6:8-9, 14(a); Genesis 7:5; Genesis 9:1

Genesis 12:1-2, 4(a); Genesis 21: 1-3; Romans 4:9(b), 16

Exodus 3:1-2, 9-10; Exodus 5:1; Exodus 12:41-42

Exodus 20:3-4, 7, 10, 12-17

Joshua 1:1-2, 11; Joshua 24:28

Genesis 32:29

Matthew 16:18-19; Acts 2:38

Acts 9:4, 15, 20; Acts 13:44, 47-48

Genesis 14:18-20; Genesis 15:1; Exodus 23:19

Deuteronomy 14:22-24; Numbers 18:21

Deuteronomy 12:11; Deuteronomy 26:12-14; Proverbs 3:9

Malachi 3:8-12; Matthew 23:21

Mark 12:42-44; Luke 21:1-4; Matthew 6:21; Luke 12:34

Psalm 24:1; 1 Corinthians 10:26

Matthew 26:36, 40

Psalm 34:1; Psalm 100: 4-5; James 1:5-6(a)

Acts 1:8; Acts: 10:42-43; Jeremiah 33:3

Scripture for Chapter Fifteen

Genesis 1:1-2; Genesis 2:1-1-3

Exodus 6:3

Luke 11:2(a); Genesis 1:27-28

Genesis 2:18, 20(b); Genesis 2:22-23; Genesis 5:2

Genesis 2:19, 20(a)

Genesis 3:20; 4:1-2(a)

Matthew 1:21; Matthew 8:16; Mark 10:1

Isaiah 7:14; Ephesians 4:11-12

Proverbs 1:1-9

John 10:10(b)

Proverbs 22:9; Malachi 3:10; Luke 6:38

Mark 4:15(b); John 10:10(a); 2 Corinthians 11:13-14

I Peter 5:8; Luke 22:3

Romans 10:9; Acts 4:12; John 14:6; Acts 16:31; Romans 10:13

Luke 15:10; John 10:29

Hebrews 10:25; Malachi 3:10-12

2 Timothy 2:15; 1 Thessalonians 5:17

Matthew 25:14-30; Revelation 20:12-13,15

ABOUT THE AUTHOR

Ms. Griggs earned a Bachelor of Arts degree in Social Science from CSU, Sacramento, California.

She retired as a Senior Probation Officer with over 30 years of experience in Juvenile and Adult Probation Services.

Currently, Ms. Griggs produces videos on genealogy and goal planning. In addition, she enjoys speaking about both secular and non-secular subjects.

Ms. Griggs belongs to a mystery book club, enjoys reading and writing in several genres, including Christian mystery novels. Her hobbies include traveling, family genealogy, and being an avid sports fan of Northern California teams. Ms. Griggs is also a novice in quilting arts and guitar.

Ms. Griggs and her family live in Northern California.

www.ingramcontent.com/pod-product-compliance
Lightning Source LLC
Chambersburg PA
CBHW070757020526
44118CB00036B/1866